LINDA WAGNER

Hope for Tomorrow

A COLLECTION OF WORDS AND IMAGES THAT WILL ENCOURAGE AND INSPIRE

Author: Linda Sue Wagner
Publisher: Xlibris, Random House Ventures,
                               L.L.C., subsidiary of Random House, Inc.
                               Xlibris Corporation, 436 Walnut Street, 11th Floor,
                               Philadelphia, PA 19106
Cover photography: Cheryl Payne, Stillwater, OK
Cover design and layout: Bruce Kittle, Blue Springs, MO
Additional photo cover
Text revisions and
Picture layout and
Original text design: Larry Lierman, Independence, Missouri

Copyright © 2019 by Linda Wagner. 545578
Library of Congress Control Number: 2003195042

ISBN: Softcover   978-1-4134-3626-6

Print information available on the last page

Rev. date: 05/07/2019

To order additional copies of this book, contact:
Xlibris
1-888-795-4274
www.Xlibris.com
Orders@Xlibris.com

FORWARD

All direct scripture quotes are quoted from the King James Version of the Bible unless otherwise stated. Scripture references to direct quotations, ideas, and paraphrases are located at the bottom of each poem. All personal pronouns and adjectives used in reference to God and Jesus are capitalized for distinction to infer reverence to God. The words for my emotional healing and my scripture message are from Psa. 30:11 "You, O' Lord, have turned my mourning into dancing" and Psa. 30:5 "Weeping cometh in the night; but joy cometh in the morning."

DEDICATION

In the past, I have shared various passages from this book with people who were going through enormous trials, in hopes that I might minister God's comfort, encouragement, and healing to them as they begin to receive hope and freedom from their pain. Many of them have later shared with me that they were greatly encouraged and comforted by the words in this book. I have, in turn, received a great blessing. My greatest desire is that those in the future would also be blessed and freed; therefore, giving this book the purpose for which it was intended. I now dedicate this book to all those who have read and benefited from my poems in the past and to all those in the present and future that suffer from great emotional pain and loss in their life, who feel that there is no hope for tomorrow. I believe that God has truly inscribed these words in my heart to show all those suffering from emotional pain that there is, yes indeed, "HOPE FOR TOMORROW."

ACKNOWLEDGEMENTS

I extend a grateful heart to all the Christians who encouraged and comforted me in my trials and assisted me in publishing this book. Below are just a few of those special people, as it is impossible to mention everyone.

To my lovely daughter, Tammy, who was always my "little bubble of joy" during difficult times, even in the midst of her own trials and my son, Bill, my "tender one", who always believed this book would be published.

To my closest friend, Connie Adaire, who has been the greatest inspiration that I have ever known, who taught me through her life what it truly means to continue to love God, while persevering against all odds.

To Evelyn Gasper, my cousin and dear friend, as well as my real estate agent who aided me in buying my home.

To my dear friend, Melanie Adams, who "hung in there" with me through the same excruciating trials and though many miles have separated us, our hearts remain closely entwined to this day.

To my dear friend, Carol Matson, who is responsible for many souls going to heaven and whose special gift of singing would always lift my up my "spirits."

To my sweet friend, Penny Ruth, who was faithful to pray with me and just enjoyed having fun with me.

To Dennis and Marilyn Carroll who were 2 of my greatest encouragers to publish this book and who were amazed that God had also broadened my vision to bless hurting people through "Beautiful Creations" items.

To Mary Haley, my counselor and friend, who helped me to put the past and "self-inflicted" guilt behind, as she said, "Today, you would respond differently, with the wisdom you have gained over the years from God."

To Pastor Howard Cordell, Faith Covenant Church, Blue Springs, MO, I'll never forget his reading my manuscript, stating that I needed art illustrations as he read "No Mountain Too High" and said, "Where are the mountains?"

To Pastor Derek Kirkman, Destiny Christian Church, who assured me that God would complete the work He had begun in my book and my business, "Beautiful Creations."

To Cheryl Payne, and Pastor John and Kathie Ware, who comforted and counseled me during the first years of the horrific emotional crisis and Mrs. Billie Fisher, a precious woman filled with enormous joy, as well as Becky Newkirk and Sharon Klingamon who always provided me with a listening ear and a place of refuge.

To Jerry and Debbie Mitchell, who were the first to befriend me at Faith Covenant Church and who lovingly extended their great wisdom to me during many difficult and confusing circumstances.

To Lynn Clark, a mighty intercessor, her daughter, Tammy Colvin, a writer and Marchetta DeVries, who equally proclaimed God's hand on this book and gave me a glimpse of hope for my business, "Beautiful Creations."

To Becky Batulicus and Ann Waldron who saw God's ministry flowing through my writings, as well as Elaine Hansen and Bonnie Bryan, whose precious friendship brightened my life in Johnstown, PA as well as many others.

HER STORY

Linda grew up on a small farm near Lamar, MO. She was a very quiet, introverted and shy little girl with a very low self-esteem. Linda experienced the death of her father when she was 19, two very emotionally traumatic marriages, the death of her second husband, her mother-in-law-her best friend, as well as the death of her own mother. She has suffered the pain of physical and emotional abuse during her first marriage to an alcoholic, physically abusive adulterer, as well as other equally painful and challenging experiences during her second marriage. During her second marriage, she and her family moved to Stillwater, OK. After 23 years and two very difficult marriages, she became a single parent at 40 years old, enduring the struggle of raising a child while working in fast food restaurants at $3.15 an hour, being virtually exhausted, almost to the point of giving up. Consequently, she sought to improve her financial "way of life" by attending secretarial vocational school at 42 years old, while still enduring emotional trauma to herself and her children. She acquired her first clerical job as a legal secretary. During her employment as a legal secretary, she was chosen by the Oklahoma Department of Human Services to deliver a speech concerning her success story to new single mothers entering the vocational training program. At age 47, she and her daughter embarked upon a major emergency move, returning to her birth state of MO, to care for her aging mother. Linda has continued a career in a variety of clerical positions. She is ever grateful to God for His faithfulness to her as He provided for her spiritually, emotionally, mentally, financially, and physically. Life has continued to have "ups and downs" for Linda; however, she has continued to persevere with a goal for "better things in the future." She is most grateful to have a Heavenly Father who will never give up on her; even when she failed, at times, to "fix her eyes" totally on Jesus during each and every traumatic circumstance. Even though Linda does not claim to have obtained to perfection spiritually, emotionally, or materially, she gives God all the praise and glory for His continuing to perfect and mature her and give her the strength to become more than a conqueror over all her trials. She attests that He has shown her that He often takes us through painful circumstances to strengthen and mature us so that we may encourage others experiencing similar circumstances. She reminisces upon her "hard times" and reflects upon the passage in the Bible, from the story of Joseph, where Joseph stated to his brothers, "What you have meant for evil, God has meant for good." She enjoys her blessings of 2 adult children: her daughter, Tammy Atterbury and her son, Bill Parker, her son-in-law, Michael Atterbury and her darling grandson, Parker Mason Atterbury. Linda acknowledges that she has learned that in God's journey, nothing is permanent and everything is "subject to change," in order that He may continue to perform His perfect work in her life (Phil.1:6). She eagerly awaits her future journeys with God. Her additional accomplishment is her business, since 12/2001, "Beautiful Creations." She attests she uses passages from this book, printing them in the sky of nature scene photographs for 8 x 10 matted-framed pictures, as well as printing poems on specialty prints for 5 x7 pictures, tabletop devotionals, daily devotional cards, refrigerator magnets, bookmarks, gift cards, note cards, and other novelty items. She has sold a large number of items at the "Master's Touch" Christian store in Warrensburg, MO. She extends thanks to her niece, Jamie Kittle for her assistance with art show assistance and item creations, as well as her great nieces, Raimah and Rachael Kittle, her daughter, Tammy, her daughter's friend, Shonte', and several pre-teen girls from Faith Covenant Church for the assembly of pictures. If you would like to know more about "Beautiful Creations," please contact Linda at: "Beautiful Creations," (816) 456-5683.

CONTENTS

HOPE FOR TOMORROW

The 'storms of tragedy', in your life, will seem to shatter all your dreams of tomorrow. In the midst of your 'difficult storms', tears will streak down your face. You might wonder what will become of your wretched life. It may be you do not have the strength to cope with the pain. You could say to Jesus, "Where are the 'rose colored-gardens?'" Perhaps, loneliness, fear, and grief will surround you. It is likely that you feel no one cares for you. They may not realize what you must endure. There is Some One, who cares deeply for you. My friend, He loves you in the midst of every painful moment you that will ever have to go through.

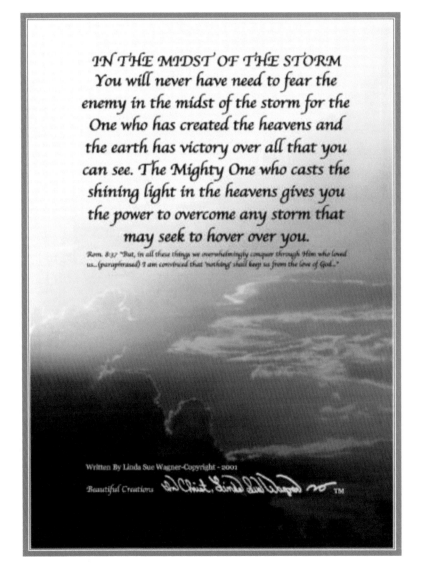

IN THE MIDST OF THE STORM
You will never have need to fear the enemy in the midst of the storm for the One who has created the heavens and the earth has victory over all that you can see. The Mighty One who casts the shining light in the heavens gives you the power to overcome any storm that may seek to hover over you.

Rom. 8:37 "But, in all these things we overwhelmingly conquer through Him who loved us...(paraphrased) I am convinced that 'nothing' shall keep us from the love of God..."

Written By Linda Sue Wagner-Copyright - 2001

Beautiful Creations ™

His name is Jesus. Jesus is the Son of the eternal loving God. He is there for you, even if it seems that there is no reason for you to look to what lies ahead. So, do not be discouraged or forlorn. Instead, I ask you to gaze your eyes upon your loving Savior, Jesus. At that time, you should cast all your burdens (cares) upon Him. Then He will burst His shining light of love into your heart. Next, He will heal your despair with His love. Afterward, He will remove all your storms of suffering and sorrow. When you reach your hand out to Jesus, He will take your hand and walk with you, throughout each day. My friend, He will come to give you His hope for tomorrow, as you encounter your greatest storm.

HIS SHINING LIGHT
Reach out to your blessed Lord, Jesus, as He bursts His shining light through your storms of sorrow. He will fill you with His abundant joy and give you that hope and a future for tomorrow. He will give you a glorious new hope and cause you to look with expectancy toward your future for tomorrow.

Isa. 60:1 "Arise, shine: for your Light has come, and the glory of the Lord has risen upon you."
Jer. 29:11 "(paraphrased) I have plans of good and not evil to give you a future and a hope."

Written By Linda Sue Wagner-Copyright - 2001   Beautiful Creations

2

My friend, when you gave Jesus the authority over yourself, you may have assumed that the life of a Christian should be stress free. I want you to know, Jesus never guaranteed you could avoid afflictions (emotional, health, or financial). *Although, He <u>did</u> promise that He would be your ever-present help in your time of need.*

Nevertheless, Satan always opposes God. Now, my friend, you must, "Be sober-minded; be watchful. (because) **Your adversary, the devil, prowls around like a roaring lion, seeking someone to devour."** *He will harass your emotions on your weakest day. At this time, he will use dread and despair to 'bring you down'. You will find they will cause much stress to your mind. When this happens, it is extremely important for you not listen to the lies of Satan.*

Yet, Jesus has come to offer you His eternal life. He also came to give you freedom (healing) *from your pain. You will need to surrender those emotions to the Lord, Jesus. He may ask you to wait patiently, as He heals you through a day-by-day process. While you wait on Him and rest in Him, He will draw you closer to Him each day. After that, He will bind up your aching wounds. It is then He will comfort and nurture your soul, with His everlasting love. Soon after, He will calm the storms and smooth the troubled waters in your life. He will hear the cry of your heart and will wipe away every tear you shed. Next, He will remove your weeping in the night. On the other hand, He could choose to 'set you free' in one miraculous moment with the touch of His mighty hand. No matter how He decides to heal you, your pain will cease. At that point, Jesus will trade your sorrows with a beautiful garment of praise. Immediately, He will turn your mourning into a dance of joy. Now, you can put on your garment of praise and the oil of gladness. This is so you will be able to sing songs of adoration unto the Lord. At this instant, you can dance before the Lord, just as David did, as the dawn dispels the night.*

As you place all your trust in your heavenly Father, you can look to the future with peace and great anticipation. After that, I ask you to listen closely to the Lord. At that time, He will speak these encouraging words to you from the Word, "For I know the plans I have for you (My child), declares the Lord, plans for welfare and not for evil, to give you a future and hope." When you think about Him and the hope He has given you; then, you will surely have a wonderful

HOPE FOR TOMORROW.

Scripture References: Ps. 30:5b, 11; Ps. 34:17-19; Ps. 46:1; Ps. 147:3; Prv. 23:18; Is. 61:3; Jer. 29:11-12; Jer. 31:13b; Lk. 4:18; Jn.14:1; Jn. 16:33; 1 Pt. 5:8

WHERE WOULD I BE?

(All my praise to God, my heavenly Father, for my salvation)

Where would I be today, if You had not found me in the depths of the sea? Where would I be today, if You had not seen my sin, forgiven me, and had mercy on me? Where would I be today, if You had not called me out of darkness and into Your marvelous light, and set me free? Where would I be today, if You had not reached Your gentle hand down from Your glorious heaven above and lovingly touched me with Your powerful love?

Where would I be today, if You had not heard my cry and had not listened to me? Where would I be today, if You had not seen the pain within me? Where would I be today, my Lord, if I had not willingly surrendered all my pain and heartache completely to You?

Where would I be today, if You had not touched me and healed me? Where would I be today, if You had not shown me who I am in You? Where would I be today, if You had not shown me the dark places in my soul? Where would I be today, if You had not set Your Holy Spirit in me or had not breathed on me? Where would I be today, if You had not spoken to me, day by day? Where would I be today, if You had not held out Your hand to me and said, "Come, My child, and follow Me, for you and I have a journey to travel together. Come and follow Me, for I have many great things to show you." Where would I be today, if I could not hear other broken hearts crying out to You? Where would I be today, if I could not fall on bended knee on their behalf, to You?

Where would I be today, if You had not rescued me from the depths of the sea and set me free? Where would I be today, if all my praise and gratitude had not gone to You, my Lord, Jesus? Could it be that, today, I would still be lost in the depths of the mighty, deep blue sea? Where would I be?" O' God, all my thanks goes to You, my Lord, Jesus.

Scripture References: 2 Sm. 22:4-6, 17, 20, 25a

RISE UP AND SMILE

At this moment, you might be viewing Satan's attack upon your mind through your feelings. This is understandable, when you are distressed. In doing so, you can become emotionally weak. When your thoughts are on the crisis, which you are struggling with; it could look bleak. As a result, you may be tempted to say, "This is not fair. These things I cannot bear!" Even so, you have to put your trust in Jesus. Then, He will keep you in His loving care; especially, when your life seems so stressful. I ask you not to look at what you are enduring. Rather, you should decide to walk by faith, instead of by your feelings, upon your rugged mile. If you do; then you <u>can</u> make the choice to rise up and smile; since, you know the Lord will <u>always</u> be with you. So, ". . . let not your heart be troubled . . . ," concerning the traumatic experience, which you are dealing with. When you are in the midst of a crisis, the Lord will give you His peace. Then He will help you to overcome the evil that is seeking to harm you. You can 'rise up and smile', for He has provided an escape for you (satisfied soul) *from the clutches of the enemy. Now, listen to the words of instruction from Him:*

"'My child, you must hold fast to what your eyes behold in My Word for I have said to you, "Trust in the Lord with all your heart, and do not lean on your own understanding. In all your ways acknowledge Him, and He will make straight your paths." When you 'lean on your own understanding;' then you will dread all that you see. When you feel alone, I, the Lord, thy God, will never forsake you. When you are weak, I will give you strength. I say to you, '. . . whatever is true, whatever is honorable, whatever is just, whatever is pure, whatever is lovely, whatever is commendable . . . ;' then, 'think about these things.' Whenever you trust Me with what concerns you, you will find rest for your soul. You must know that all I do for you is for your best.'"

There is a story in the Bible, about a man named Joseph, whose brothers betrayed him. It would have been easy for him not to forgive them. Even so, he chose to 'rise up and smile' and to forgive his brothers. He knew that God had a bigger plan for his life, his brothers, and all the people in the land. When you come to the point of facing your circumstances by faith; then, rejoice in what God will do for you, just as Joseph did. I implore you to rise up and smile; then, trust Jesus in every possible way. Now, the grace of God will shine upon your face just as He has caused the golden sun to shine upon this lake.

IMMEASURABLY MORE

Just as the creator of the heavens and the earth can cause the radiant sunlight to be cast upon this beautiful lake, so shall He do immeasurably more in your life than you can even comprehend. His Holy Spirit will show you that His vast love has no end and that He will make everything right in your life for His name's sake.

Eph. 3:20 "Now to Him who is able to do exceeding abundantly beyond all that we ask or think according to the power that works within us..." Rom. 8:26 "All things work together..."

Written By Linda Sue Wagner - Copyright -2001
Beautiful Creations

When you put your trust in God, He promises that He will do immeasurably more for you, far beyond, what you can comprehend. He will surely work out His purpose in your life. My friend, when He does that, it is solely for His glorious name's sake.

Let us examine the faith of another man, in the Bible. His name was David. He knew the mighty strength of the hand of the heavenly Father would preserve (protect) him, in all of his life threatening predicaments. Thus, he faced his fearful conditions with great boldness. So, he chose to 'rise up and smile' in the middle of some of his most harrowing battles. He, also, chose to 'rise up and smile' during his darkest moments of the night. This was because he sang songs of praise to the Lord for everything he had already done for him and for what he knew God was going to do. You can face your most fearful times with the same attitude that David and Joseph had. When you do, then your soul will 'rise up and smile', too. When you think on the marvels of the Lord, just as David did; then, you can voice songs of praise to Him.

It is not good to look back into your past or let your thoughts dwell upon the dilemma that brings you despair. When you focus on what you see, it is certain your smile will not last. So, do not let your soul feel utterly cast down and without hope. Instead, you should place your dependence, totally in Him, who sings songs of deliverance over you. Then, He will be with you through the deep waters of much trouble. When you walk in the great fires (painful events), they will not burn you up. As you rise up and smile, in one of the most challenging stages you have ever dealt with; Jesus will give you His assurance of victory over your negative thoughts, which only He can give. If you wear a smile on your face; rather than a frown, all those who see you will know that you look to the time, which is still to come and not upon the past. God will give you a joy far beyond what the world can possibly give. He will pour out His grace upon all He has given you. When you let Jesus walk with you each day, you can look forward to an eternity with Him; then, your struggles will only be for a 'little while'.

Scripture References: Gn. 37:3-4, 23-28; Gn. 39:1, 20; Gn. 41:1, 15-16, 39-40; Gn. 45:7-8; Gn. 50:20-21; Ps. 32:7; Ps. 63:6; Prv. 3:5-6; Is. 43:2; Jn. 14:27; 1 Cor. 10:13c; 2 Cor. 4:18; 2 Cor. 5:7; Eph. 3:20; Phil. 4:8

THE RED SEA

When you react to a gravely worrisome disaster in fear and lack of faith in God, you can become just as overwhelmed as the people of Israel were when they looked upon the raging Red Sea. You might look at your 'red sea' (problems), saying to God in dismay, "Lord, I cannot find a way to pass through my 'red sea'. Can You still part the 'red sea' in my life?" I assure you; if you put your trust in God, you will see He is so mighty that even today, He can divide the waters of the 'red sea' in your life. Look at what God, the heavenly Father, did to the Red Sea through the faith of Moses. His faith was one of the greatest examples of trust in God, ever portrayed in the Bible. By faith, he trusted God. Through his faith in God, he could see far beyond what the doubtful people of Israel could, as they stood and looked at their Red Sea, with intense fear. Then, they were ungrateful towards God. The Israelites reacted to what they saw in rebellion (discord and complaining). However, Moses put his trust in God. He knew that when he lifted up his staff, God's mighty hand would divide the raging waters of the great Red Sea, which stood between them and their Promised Land. At that time, they walked safely through the Red Sea.

If you are staring at the 'red sea' in your life with fear, defeat, and distrust in God; then, they will control you, just as they did the people of Israel. That could even change the direction of your life, even as it did for that generation. The heavenly Father desires for you to look beyond your 'red sea' and trust Him, even as Moses did; rather than living in hopeless defeat. When you put all your trust in Him, He will make Himself known to you in the same way, as He did for Moses. As you glean this truth from the Bible, you will see how God revealed Himself, through the miracle of the Red Sea. This is so you can see His awesome power and wondrous majesty.

When you put all your trust in Him, He will make Himself known to you, just as He did for Moses. Now, I encourage you to listen to God, as He proclaims to you:

"'Did I not I part the Red Sea for the Israelites? Is there anything impossible for Me? There is always hope for you as you look to Me to part your Red Sea. Do not be dismayed as you stand before your 'red sea'. I have thrown the horse and rider into the sea. Therefore, you can now rejoice in the victory you will have in Me as I part your 'red sea'. Then, you can shout a new song of joy, just as Miriam did when she sang and danced with her tambourine, *"I will sing to the Lord, for He has triumphed gloriously; the horse and his rider He has thrown into the sea."'*

Scripture References: Ex. 14:1-31; Ex. 15:1-19; 21; Psa. 106:7-13; Phil. 2:14

THE GREAT PROVIDER

My friend, for many people limited finances can become a great drain upon their life. When you look at your financial needs and see no provision to meet them; then, it can cause anxiety and discouragement. You may cry out to God saying, "I do not have enough money to feed my family, or meet their needs."

When your thoughts are fearful, you may think, "In my mind I cannot find a way to cope. I do not realize that there is a reason to have hope." Despite what you are experiencing, I ask you to look at it with the wisdom of Christ. Then, you will be able to receive the assurance that He will always provide a way to meet your every need.

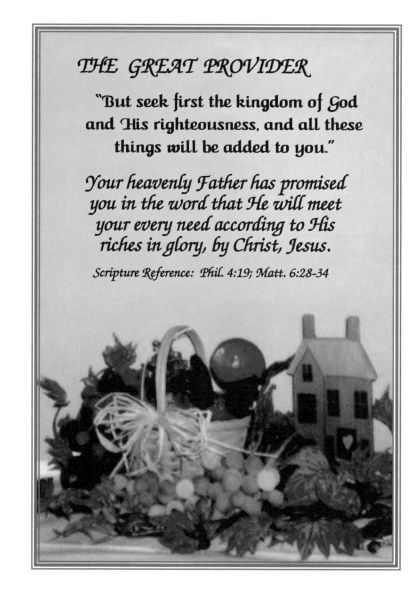

THE GREAT PROVIDER

"But seek first the kingdom of God and His righteousness, and all these things will be added to you."

Your heavenly Father has promised you in the word that He will meet your every need according to His riches in glory, by Christ, Jesus.

Scripture Reference: Phil. 4:19; Matt. 6:28-34

Dear one, as you seek the heavenly Father and come before Him with a humble heart, He will speak these words of assurance to you:

"My child, when you trust Me, I will bless you, even in your moment of weakness. I only ask that you have the same attitude as the widow had, when she only had enough meal to feed herself and her son; yet, she fed my servant. Therefore, I bountifully met their need. When you delight yourself in Me, I will share with you, all the riches of My kingdom. So, do not allow the bread you seek to become more important to you than hearing My voice. You must desire to hear My voice before having your needs met.'"

I also ask you to consider the words that Jesus has spoken from the Word:

"'. . . do not be anxious about your life, what you will eat, or what you will drink, nor about your body, what you will put on.' . . . 'And which of you by being anxious can add a single hour to his span of life? And why are you anxious about clothing? Consider the lilies of the field, how they grow; they neither toil nor spin, yet I tell you, even Solomon in all his glory was not arrayed like one of these. But if God so clothes the grass of the field, which today is alive and tomorrow is thrown into the oven, will He not much more clothe you, O you of little faith? Therefore, do not be anxious saying, 'What shall we eat?' or 'What shall we drink?' or 'What shall we wear?' . . . your heavenly Father knows that you need them all. But seek first the kingdom of God and His righteousness, and all these things will be added to you."

At this point, I beckon you to focus your thoughts on the blessed Savior, Jesus, and His perfect peace, for He promised that He would bountifully meet all your needs.

I say to you, dear one, "Will He not do so much more, for whom His delight is in?" So, present all your needs to your heavenly Father, with a committed heart. Then you can say to Him, "To You only, Lord, will I choose to yield my heart."

Now, place your trust in the heavenly Provider, then lift up your hands toward Him, with all your heart. After that, He will lift your "spirits" up higher. At that time, you will rest securely, when you know He "... will supply every need of yours according to His riches in glory in Christ Jesus." He will, surely do that for you, because all His delight is focused on you.

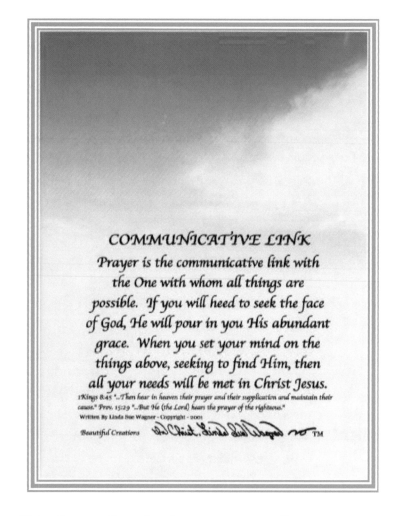

COMMUNICATIVE LINK

Prayer is the communicative link with the One with whom all things are possible. If you will heed to seek the face of God, He will pour in you His abundant grace. When you set your mind on the things above, seeking to find Him, then all your needs will be met in Christ Jesus.

1Kings 8:45 "...Then hear in heaven their prayer and their supplication and maintain their cause." Prov. 15:29 "...But He (the Lord) hears the prayer of the righteous."

Written By Linda Sue Wagner - Copyright - 2001

Beautiful Creations   ™

Dear one, you no longer need to walk in fear. His Word assures you; His greatest desire is to meet your every need, beyond your imagination! Now is the time to give Him the praise He is due!

Scripture References: Ex. 16:3a-4; Dt. 8:3b-4; 1 Kgs. 17:3-16; 1 Kgs 19:4-8; Mt. 4:4; Mt. 6:25-34; Mt. 7:7-8; Mk. 8:2-9; Phil. 4:19

JESUS CARES

Dear one, when you are suffering the loss of a loved one, the grief and sorrow are especially difficult to go through. In your grief and despair, you may cry out to Jesus, and say, "I cannot bear this grief alone! Why did I have to lose my loved one?" I cannot give you an answer, for there is not an answer here on this earth. If your loved one has received Jesus as their Savior, someday you will join that one in heaven. I want you to know that you do not have to handle this grief alone. Jesus will come to you as the great Comforter. He came to comfort Mary and Martha after their brother Lazarus died. With His abundant compassion, He will send people to put their arms around you, as they comfort you. As they comfort you, He will, in time; remove your tears and give you good memories. When you feel alone in the loss of your loved one you must remember, He will always be with you. Believe me; I share your pain, from the loss of my beloved son. 1st Peter 5:7 states ". . . casting (cast) all your anxieties (painful emotions) on Him, because He cares (very deeply) for you." I beckon you to open your heart to receive the love, comfort, and compassion the Lord will pour into your soul in your time of pain and loss. Listen to Him, as He holds you in His arms, saying:

"My child, you may feel there is no comfort for your grief. I am 'acquainted with your grief', for I carry the grief of the world. I care about all your emotions, during the loss of your loved one. 'I, I am He who comforts you; . . . .' Your loved one's new home is a far greater place than anything I created on earth. That one begins a new life with Me, forever. Now, their joy will be unspeakable. After I comfort you and heal your aching heart, then you can comfort others who grieve the loss of a loved one."

Scripture References: Is. 51:12a; Is. 53:4a; Is. 61:2c; Jer. 31:13b; Mt. 5:4; 2 Cor. 1:3-4; 1 Pt. 5:7

NEVER WALK ALONE IN YOUR JOURNEY OF FAITH

When you began your journey of faith, you may not have known it would be so hard. It is not always emotionally comfortable to walk the journey of faith, which is set before you. As you walk forward, you might struggle with many types of tough challenges. Then, Satan, your enemy, will come to you in an unguarded instant. He is the master of deception and the father of lies. He walks in darkness so you cannot see him. His plan is to deceive your mind and blind you to his evil lies. His objective is to wear down your confidence in God. If he succeeds, you will not be able to receive the heavenly Father's love, power, and direction. Satan's first plot is to make you to feel, God does not care about you. He attempts to make you take your eyes off the Lord, so you will not sense His presence in your life. Next, you will feel like you are all alone. If he can convince you that it is true, you will believe there is no hope. Then, you will not be able to cope with his plans to devastate you. When you only look at your troubles, you might feel you will never be free of them. If you believe Satan's lies, he will accomplish his final goal to lure you away from your trust in your heavenly Father. You might cry out to Him in the midst of dread and loneliness, saying, "I cannot walk this road alone. I am not strong enough!" Walking the journey of faith can be rough. It is not the Lord's desire for you to walk alone. His desire is for you to walk beside Him and let Him carry the horrible encumbrance (burden) in your life. There are times on your journey of faith, when you will not know the right path to follow. At this point, you will need to ask the Lord for His wisdom and direction, by prayer and abiding in the Word. As you seek Him, you will hear Him saying to you, "'And your ears will hear a word behind you, saying, 'This is the way, walk in it,' when you turn to the right or when you turn to the left.'"

My friend, as you look ahead, I want you to know your heavenly Father desires for you to walk right by His side, in the cool breeze of the morning. He walked with Adam and Eve, before their sin caused them to turn away from Him. For that reason, they could no longer sense God's presence. If you reject Him, the path of your journey will be just as troublesome and grievous as it was for Adam and Eve. Instead, I ask you to listen carefully to the heavenly Father for His direction. When you are too exhausted to fight your battles, you must "... Be of strong and courageous ...." You can, because your mighty Savior stands by your side to fight your enemy.

Dear one, it is imperative for you to read the book of Psalms to discover David's approach to what terrified him. He was a man who sought to follow 'hard' after the Lord, with all his heart, his mind, and strength. This was in the midst of his most, harrowing, times of combat with the enemy. If you want to walk in the might of the Lord, then you must seek Him in the same manner, as did God's beloved David.

One of Satan's greatest devises is to control you with intense worry. When he does, then you will be afraid of what lies ahead of you. In spite of your thoughts of fretfulness, I encourage you to say to Satan, "I will not be frightened or disheartened by what lies ahead of me, nor behind me." My friend, it is at this point, you can walk without dread of the unknown, as God speaks these words to you, "fear not, for I am with you; ...." "... I will never leave you, nor forsake you." He protects you, behind and before you, just as He did the Israelites at the Red Sea. Even in the midst of great anguish, David boldly affirmed his confidence in God, as he stated in Psalms, "Though I walk in the midst of trouble, You preserve my life; You stretch out Your hand against the wrath of my enemies, and Your right hand delivers me." God is always with you as He guides your way on your journey of faith. I tell you; half the battle is totally trusting in Him. When you do that; then, you have already won your battle.

When the almighty God walks with you, you do not have to be afraid of what your adversary; Satan, will do to you. Do not look at your predicament with a negative 'frame of mind'. Rather, you must walk by faith in Him, according to what you read in the Bible. When you do, you will be courageous in the midst of every trial that Satan may try to 'throw in your face'. The Lord will always be your shield and protector, your guide, comfort, and strength. With His shield of faith, you <u>*can be a mighty warrior or warrioress.*</u> *You can have a calm soul when you know the Lord walks with you, every day. At that time, you can walk in the light of the Lord. So, dear one, you must come to the place where your greatest desire is to magnify and exalt Him with exuberant thanksgiving; for He is the One who walks ahead of you and beside you, every step of the way, on your journey of faith.*

Scripture References: Dt. 31: 6-8; Jos. 1:9a; Ps. 50:11; Ps. 56:13; Ps. 69:30; Ps. 138:7; Ps. 139: 5; Ps. 143: 8b; Is. 2:5; Is 30:21; Is. 41:10; 2 Cor. 5:7; Heb. 13:5

JESUS, YOUR ABIDING REFUGE

My friend, there are times in which you must face a brutal assault from Satan. In the midst of your feelings of fearfulness and gloom, you may feel there is no one to help you. If you suppose that to be true; then, it might be easy for you to fall prey to the devious voice of Satan. When you heed to the voices of terror and despair you are not listening to the Lord. You are listening to Satan, the deceiver. He will whisper lies in your ear. Then, he will try to 'tear you down'. He will tell you that there is no chance for you to be free from this onslaught. He will then make you feel like you have no place to hide. At this time, you could begin to feel, utterly, cast headlong (down). *Next, you might wear a frown upon your face. You do not have to accept Satan's evil lies, for He is the one who walks in darkness. When despairing emotions seem to overwhelm you, you must call upon Jesus, your abiding refuge. His refuge is the only place where you can find true safety. He will always be faithful to you in the midst of your greatest fears. He will show you His love by enfolding His arms around you, as if He were a dove from the shining heavens above. When you kneel at His feet, His mighty arms will embrace you with His loving-kindness and abundant grace. So, listen to Him as He gently speaks these words of wisdom to you:*

"'My child, sit and listen; then, you will hear me, when I tell you I am your Abiding Refuge. Do not regret that which has brought you much pain, because it has driven you to rest in the security of My everlasting arms of protection. Trust Me at all times. Then I will pour peace into your soul and give you blessed rest on every side. When you realize that I am here with you, you cannot be utterly, cast down. As soon as I give you My peace, Satan cannot take it away. Even so, you will have to endure many battles in this life.

I am your Most High God, your fortress (high tower of strength) and your hiding place. I will hide you from the trouble the enemy brings. When you seek My abiding refuge (the Shelter of the Most High God), I will deliver you from the snare of the fowler. I will take away your weakness and make you steadfast and strong. I have crushed his head under My feet. Now, you do not have to dread Satan. When you realize that I have stomped him to the ground, you can rejoice. You are in My everlasting care; therefore, no one or nothing can destroy your spirit. I will fill your heart with joy and surround you with songs of deliverance. At this time, you can let your voice rise up with a song of praise to My Holy name, just like My beloved David did. You will rest under the everlasting arms of My abiding refuge, for I have victory over all your enemies. Therefore, you do not need to fear. You must confidently proclaim, with great joy to those who would have ears to hear, *'My God will do valiantly, for in Him, I will have the ultimate victory, over the enemy.'"*

In the midst of your greatest fears, your abiding refuge will always be faithful to you. You can now rejoice, for your suffering soul will find a quiet rest and a safe place with God, where you can hide from the enemy.

Scripture References: Dt. 33:27; Ps. 18:2; Ps. 32:7; Ps. 46:1; Ps. 60:12; Ps. 61:3; Ps. 62:8; Ps. 91:1-3; Ps. 118:15; Is. 41:10; Jer. 16:19a; Rom. 16:20

WHAT TIME I AM AFRAID

It is not always easy to be strong in the midst of, possibly, your most severely stressful traumas. You know the Word says you should have faith like a mustard seed. Yet, fear and doubt can still creep deep into your thoughts. This could cause your faith to waver. During your despair, you may say to God, "I am afraid I do not have enough faith for You to answer my prayers!" When you are afraid and your eyes are full of tears, you might wonder if the heavenly Father still loves you. I urge you not to allow Satan to cause you to feel condemned for your lack of faith. God knows your heart is true to Him. If there is fear and doubt in your mind, then I challenge you to read the Word. At that time, you can learn how some of the great people of faith dealt with their fears. So, trust Him with the things that test your faith, just as those people did. Then, you will find that He will give you His peace, instead of fear. This is as He did for Elijah, Job, David, Peter, and many others.

Elijah was a mighty prophet of God. The Lord sent him to tell His people of the things to come. He said there would be no rain for three years. This devastated the land of Israel. He told Elijah to destroy all the evil prophets, so he did. Queen Jezebel then threatened his life. He became very fearful of her and fled to the mountains. Yet, God met him there and drew him back to Him in a powerful way.

Satan told God, Job would turn away from Him, if he took everything from him. God told Satan that He knew Job would remain faithful to Him. Thus, God allowed Satan to take Job's family, his health, and wealth. In Job's grief, he cried out to God and said to Him, "For the thing that I feared (most) comes upon me." As a result, he suffered intense agony, in body and soul.

However, he still did not give up his faith in God. He continued to remain faithful to Him. As a result, He restored everything back to Job that Satan had taken.

As you deal with fear, you will receive insight, in the Bible, from the life of a man named David. He loved and trusted his heavenly Father, dearly. Nevertheless, there were many times in which he went through colossal periods of apprehension and hopelessness. In one of those matters, he cried out, even as Jesus did, "My God, my God, why have You forsaken me?" However, even in the midst of his doubts and fears, he rose up with all of his might and affirmed, "When I am afraid, I will put my trust in You . . . ." and "Some trust in chariots, and some in horses; but we (I will) trust in the name of our God." He was positive that the heavenly Father would always be there for him. David knew that God would defeat (Satan), his terrorist. Thus, he spoke with great confidence, "Though an army may encamp against me, (all round me) my heart will not fear; though war arise against me; yet, I will be confident," (that) ". . . He will hide me in His shelter in the day of trouble; . . . ." The Word shows the heavenly Father had deep compassion for David. Still, there were times when he viewed the chaos in his life with fear and tear filled eyes. Yet, he was positive God was his sole protection. When he cried to Him for comfort and confidence, it was as if He was holding him in His arms saying, "I seek to bless you, even if you feel your hope looks bleak. I will hold you up if you are weak. If tears streak down your face, I will put them in My bottle."

Peter was one of Jesus' greatest followers. He walked and talked with Jesus, daily. Nevertheless, Peter did experience fear amidst his times of turmoil. When Jesus was walking on the water, Peter beckoned Jesus to let him come out onto the water with Him. However, when Peter attempted to walk out on the water to meet his Master, his fear caused him to fall beneath the water. Although, Peter had an instance of fear, he knew Jesus was there to help him.

When he fell beneath the water, he cried out, "Lord save me!" Jesus stretched out His mighty hand and pulled Peter up from the water and said, "O you of little faith, why did you doubt?" As He grasped Peter's hand, it was as if He were saying, "Even in the midst of your fear, I am here." Peter suffered moments of fear in his times of turmoil. Even so, Jesus knew Peter would become a mighty man of faith. He knew that, for when Jesus asked the disciples, "Who do you say that I am?" Peter said, "You are the Christ, the Son of the living God." As a Christian, God calls you to live life by faith in the Lord. Yet, if you feel your faith is powerless, Jesus will still lovingly reach out His hand to you in your times of fear, just as He did for Peter. Now, my friend; when you know your faith is weak, do not receive fear from the 'evil one', as Peter did.

Instead, listen to the Lord. Then, He will speak these encouraging words into your soul, "Do not be afraid of what you see with your eyes. I am with you. I will never forsake you. I have spoken to you from the Word, " . . . fear not, for I am with you; be not dismayed, for I am your God; I will strengthen you, I will help you . . . ." Dear one, do not trust in your emotions. If you do, you, most assuredly, will be terrified from the calamity that has 'come upon' your life. Fear, instead of faith, could also cause you to wonder what might happen to you in the future. You might even begin to question where God is in the midst of your challenging conditions. I can tell you; He is definitely there! I would imagine there were some people in the Bible who felt the same way. Consequently, I urge you to listen to His voice, as you diligently seek out His truths in the Word, with an open, searching, and trusting heart. At this time, His grace will show you that He abides in you, always. It is not God's will for you to walk in fear. It is His will for you to live your life by faith in Him. So, put your hope in Him in all your ways and in all your days. Then, you will look into your Savior's eyes with joy, as He lovingly looks upon your face. As you read the Word, He will show you that when you trust in Him, you can " . . . walk by faith, not by sight."

Dear one, it is of the greatest significance that you always remember to seek to rejoice in the Lord. This is especially, when you are weak. That is because, at some point in your life, you may have to face an adversity in which you might respond to with intense anxiety. At that time, my friend, I ask you to praise your beloved Savior for all that He will do for you. At this moment, dear one, you can break forth with great shouts of joy and proclaim, "I will choose not to fear what I see with my eyes. Instead, ". . . we (I will) **trust in the name of our God."**

Scripture References: Ex. 13:18-22; Ex. 14:10-13; I Kgs. 17:1; I Kgs. 18:1, 40, 1 Kgs 19:2-3, 8, 12; Job 1:1-22; Job 2:1-13; Job 3:1-25; Job 13:15; Ps. 8:6; Ps. 20:7; Ps. 22:1; Ps. 27:1, 3, 5; Ps. 56:3, 8-11; Is. 41:10; Mt. 14:22-33; Mt. 16:15-17; Mk. 8:29; 2 Cor. 5:7; Heb. 13:5b

OUR ANCHOR

My, friend, there will always be times, when you will have to deal with some awful things, which could be from the past or in the present. It is certain you will need an anchor to keep you steady in distressful times. At this time, you might feel like you are in a boat; being tossed around on the waves of the deep blue ocean, without an anchor to hold you down. When you look at the stormy waves of life's tests, Satan can attempt to mislead you with his lies. When you are in the middle of the storms of life, he will deceive you. That will cause you to feel as if you are going to sink to the bottom of the ocean, into the brink of despair. He could also seek to make you think there is nothing safe to hold onto. This is especially when you feel God is not there. Dear one, do not listen to Satan's lies, for he will try to destroy your soul.

An anchor is dependable, steadfast, and something strong to hold onto, when your life is a disaster. The Bible states that Jesus is your sure Hope of Salvation, your Firm Foundation, and the Anchor of your soul. Therefore, you must let Him be your Anchor. When you seek Jesus, He will be the Anchor who will help you with the disturbances, which has befallen you. He will give you His guidance to help you make decisions through every life-shifting change you will ever encounter. As you spend time alone with Jesus, you will know that He is your Anchor. He will make you feel secure in the traumatic seasons of your life. Then, He will not let you drift out to sea. Instead, He will be the Anchor that will keep you firmly grounded. He is the Anchor that will give you security and hope for your distressed soul. He will be there for you, when your emotions are unstable, in all the storms in your life.

Scripture References: Heb. 6:19

THE GREAT COMFORTER

My friend, at this time, you may be suffering greatly from a lengthy occurrence, which causes your life to be more complicated than it was before. You may wonder if there are better times ahead for you. Sometimes people tell you that things are going to be all right. Yet, it does not happen. Satan will tell you they do not understand your pain. It is possible that you do not know how to get through it. You may feel you will never be free from emotional or physical pain. It is then, you could think, "Why has this happened to me? Why do people not see my pain?" First, he will try to isolate you from the friends who could help you. After that, you will begin to 'shut' them out of your life. You might become weak and unable to cope with the ordeal. His following tactic is to cause you to feel that there is no one to turn to for comfort. After this, you might not find comfort from anyone. Thus, the enemy has succeeded in his plan. This could possibly bring you to a place of loneliness and utter depression. I understand, for I have had my share of grievous and dreadfully painful times.

My friend, when you put your hope in God, He will bring people into your life that have had similar struggles. They will understand your pain and be like Jesus to you. They can give you their testimony of how God gave them victory over their pain. As your friends seek to help you, they will point you to Jesus, the great Comforter. Through His compassion, He will hear your helpless cry of agony, within the silence of your soul. When you tell the Lord about your feelings of torture, He will listen to you as you say to Him, "God, I need to feel Your comfort. I must know that I am not alone. Let me hear that Your voice of comfort, encouragement, and wisdom is just a whisper away." When you are anxious and distressed, do not fret. His peace will sustain you, through every, heart wrenching ordeal.

I ask you to listen carefully, as your loving Father comforts you with this passage:

"I promised the disciples, I would leave them My Comforter. My child, I have also given <u>you</u> My Comforter. You do not have to bear all this weight of your yoke in your own strength. I will be your burden bearer. I will give you My yoke, for it is light. Do not be dismayed for I am always with you. When I take you in the shelter of My loving arms, you will receive My comfort to soothe your wrenching pain and make you free, again. Look to Me and do not lean on your own awareness with what you feel. I am always in you. You are always in Me."

My friend, do not let your soul be grieved. Rather, I ask you to receive comfort from these verses of encouragement in the Word:

"'I, I am He who comforts you;' ...' '... You will seek Me and find Me (pray to Me), when you seek Me with all your heart. I will be found by you, declares the Lord,' '... Come to Me, all who labor and are heavy laden, and I will give you rest. Take My yoke upon you, and learn from Me, for I am gentle and lowly in heart, and you will find rest for your souls.'"

I want you to know that your pain has not been in vain. The Lord will establish His purpose in every painful change in your life. I ask you to explore the greatest Biblical example of one who would survive unbearable pain and still discover God's character and purpose for his pain. <u>That man would be Job</u>. He endured an intensity of grief, which many of us will never know. He lost all his family, health, and wealth in a 'blink of an eye'. He found no comfort for his grief from anyone. He did not find comfort for his grief, especially from his emotionally distraught wife, nor from his pompous friends. They did everything; that was, except comfort him. She pleaded with him from her frustrated and distrusting soul, to curse God and die.

Though Job's grief reached far beyond any description of words, he still stood strong in his integrity and trust in God. We must admire Job for his honor, since he did not speak a word of sin with his lips. Regardless of his emotional and physical pain, he replied to her with boldness, "Shall we receive good from God, and shall we not receive evil (adversity)?" ". . . Though He slay me, I will hope in Him (and rise up and praise His awesome holy name)." He had many unbearable moments of weakness as he cried out to his heavenly Father in intense anguish, "My spirit is broken, my days are extinct; the graveyard is ready for me." ". . . Where then is my hope? Who will see my hope?" In the midst of his sorrow, Job boldly declared, "For I know that my Redeemer lives, and at the last, He will stand upon the earth; And after my skin has been thus destroyed, yet in my flesh I shall see God, whom I shall see for myself, and my eyes shall behold, and not another. My heart faints within me (for Him)!" His contentious friends accused him of sin. After that, they suggested God should take out His aggression toward Job. In spite of their criticism, he stood strong and defended his trust in God. He also forgave those who judged him. As a result, He restored everything back to Job that Satan had taken from him. You may relate to Job, as this is the cry of a disquieted heart in pain. Perhaps, there are people in your life that act like Job's friends. That is because they do not understand what the Lord is going to do in your life. If you feel Satan is torturing you, as he did Job; then, it is vital for you to rely on God's power and Job's declaration of strength in the almighty heavenly Father, as he spoke out to his critical friends. While Job sought Him for comfort and wisdom, he found that he learned more about the great Creator than he had ever known before. He realized God was all wise and most powerful. He knew He had a reason for everything that happened to him. Job was faithful to God even in the midst of his pain. So, do not be discouraged when arduous (hard) times come your way. God desires for you to seek His wisdom and comfort in the midst of the traumatic events of your life, just as Job did.

Then, Jesus will touch your heart and remove your emotional pain and bitterness. When He has healed you of your pain, then He will show you that His purpose for your pain may be that your testimony will help that 'special someone else who is hurting'. Then, He will lead you to that person. First, you must tell them how much Jesus loves them. This is so that they will know that He will comfort them, far more than you can. When they are comforted, they will be able to reach out to others who are experiencing grief. It is then that He will show His love and kindness to others, who are experiencing grief or other painful situations.

Scripture References: Job 1:21b; Job 2:9-10; Job 3:25; Job 5:7-8; Job 13:15a; Job 17:1, 15; Job 19:25-27; Job 42:1-6; Ps. 18:6; Ps. 55:22; Ps. 77:1-2; Ps. 81:6-8; Ps. 86:6-7; Is. 51:12a; Jer. 29:12-13; Na. 1:13b; Mt. 11:28-30; Jn. 14:27; 2 Cor. 1:3-4

PRECIOUS THOUGHTS

My friend, when you are dealing with the 'battles of life,' it is possible to let your mental 'guard' down. At this time, it might be hard for you to keep your thoughts upon Jesus. Satan's goal is to weaken your mind so that you will be powerless. At this point, he will cause you to reflect upon your sin, insecurities, rejections, and regrets in life. When you look at the disarray in your life, you might suppose that you are under a curse. Then, you can feel that it cannot get any worse! After that, you may feel you are of no use to anyone. If Satan can cause you to feel that you are worthless, you will assume, you are not worthy of the Lord's abounding love. It is then that you will think God could not possibly love you. My friend, this is not true! His Word states your worth to Him is dependent only upon His beloved Son's shed blood sacrifice upon the cross for all your sins. For that reason, you must not think destructive thoughts about yourself. When you read Psalms, you will find David was certain of his immense worth to his heavenly Father. In Psalms 139:14-15a, he voiced his confidence in the Lord's love for him, as he said to Him, "I praise You, for I am fearfully and wonderfully made. Wonderful are your works; my soul knows it very well. My frame was not hidden from You, when I was being made in secret, ..." As you read the Word, you will realize the vast love Jesus has for you. He delights in your enormous worth to Him. He expresses His deep love for you by saying, "All My delight is in you." You can rejoice; for the Lord has your name eternally engraved on the palm of His hand.

He desires for you to realize how marvelous His love is for you. He speaks of His powerful love for you, in Romans 8: 38-39, " . . . I am sure that neither death nor life, nor angels nor rulers, nor things present, nor things to come, nor powers, nor height nor depth, nor anything else in all creation, will be able to separate us from the love of God in Christ Jesus, our Lord." Dear one, His love is so enduring that He promises never to leave you.

Dear one, as you read the Word of God, you will see, because of His great love for you, the Lord keeps you close to Him. It is the Lord's desire for you to rest securely in His peaceful love for you. Now, I ask you to listen to the voice of the loving heavenly Father, as He expresses His endearing love for you. He sings songs of great delight over you, as He holds you in His arms and quiets your soul with His gentle love. I ask you to take great joy in realizing that through His miraculous love, He has chosen you as His inheritance. I am sure you will be convinced of His remarkable love for you, as you listen carefully to the words of the heavenly Father, when He lovingly expresses His precious thoughts toward you:

"My child, it is because of My deep love for you that I spared not the life of My very own, dearly beloved Son. When you accepted the sacrifice of My Son, I made you a brand new creation and beautiful in My sight. I have loved you with an everlasting love. I have drawn you unto Myself. Your name is eternally, carved upon the palm of My hand. My thoughts are precious and full of peace towards you. I cherish you as the apple of My eye, even as I did David. I give you an anticipated hope of glory. When you live your life for Me, your victory will be won."

Dear one, His thoughts are precious toward you. Therefore, you can rest securely in His amazing love for you. Now, live out your life with an attitude of joy, even in the midst of your toughest experiences.

Scripture References: Dt. 32:10b; Ps. 17:8; Ps. 18:19; Ps. 139:14-15; Is. 26:3; Is. 49:16; Jer. 29:11; Jer. 31:3; Zep. 3:17; Rom. 8:37-39; 2 Cor. 5:17

O' CHILD OF MINE

(Referring to every Christian as sons and daughters of the heavenly Father)

During your times of distress, your heavenly Father longs for you to come and sit at His feet and cry out to Him. In His compassion for you, He would speak these words of instruction to you:

"O' child of Mine, be not down-trodden, frightened, and in turmoil, as Satan seeks to put you beneath the soil. I have heard your cry of desperation and I have been there in the midst of all your times of dread. I have seen the misery you have suffered throughout all your years. When you thought *'I'll never be able to make it'*, I poured My Holy Spirit into your heart. I have held you in My arms as I sought to keep you safe from all that would seek to bring you to despair. When you have been weak, I have comforted you and taken away all your fears. I assure you; I deeply delight in you, because, you are cherished in My sight. I gave up the life of My own precious Son as the sacrifice for your sins, through His crucifixion. That was so you could spend an Eternity with Me. How much more could I do to show you how deeply I love and cherish you? Now, weep no more. I say to you that there is a time to weep, and a time to stand up and fight the good fight of faith. This is the time to fight! You cannot do these things by your might alone. It is by My Spirit, not by your power, nor by your might, that you will have victory over the enemy. I have taken you out of your Egypt, led you through your wilderness, and shown you the Promised Land. I have given you every weapon to defeat the enemy, especially the blood of My beloved Son. This was so I could prepare you to be of use for My glory. I have stood before you and held out My weapons to you. Thus far, you have not yet taken them to possess your promised land. This is not a time for flight, My child; but it is a time for a mighty, victorious fight!

My child, I have told you that now is the moment to fight! Have I not brought you this far? Therefore, how can you stand at the brink of your awaited promised land and say to Me, *'I do not have the strength to stand!'* Be strong in your faith. Stand up and be a victorious one. Throw aside every encumbrance that so easily entangles you. Then, prepare for the battle that is set before you! I have given you My Word and poured My Holy Spirit into you, so you can fight the enemy in all that you do. When the enemy seeks to come into your camp (your mind) to make havoc of your soul; then, you must rise up and seek Me for your battle instructions. With all My authority, you must take a stand against Satan and command him to flee from you, for I assured you in My Word, "*For though we walk in the flesh, we are not waging war according to the flesh. For the weapons of our warfare are not of the flesh, but have divine power to destroy strongholds.*" I have given you My authority, My name, the blood of My very own Son, My armor, My Word (which is the sword of the Spirit), and more, in order that your victory would be won. I assure you; the greatest battle against Satan you will ever face was all ready won, at the cross. That was when My Beloved Son arose from the grave. That stripped the enemy of the power over your soul. Now, it is up to you to victoriously rise up and boldly conquer (possess) your long awaited glorious promised land! Thus, I urge you to heed to My voice as I speak these words to you, 'Your faith and My weapons of warfare are all that you will need to drive the enemy from your midst. You must take My hand. Then, you will walk victoriously with all I that have given you, possessing all My strength. At this time, you can boldly march forward into battle to possess your promised land! O' child of Mine, take a firm stand on My solid rock; for all other ground is, surely, sinking sand!'" At this moment, you can be a joyous one.

Scripture References: Ex. 14:14; Jos. 23:3, 5; Is. 54:17; Hb. 3:17-19; Zec. 4:6b; 2 Cor. 10:4; Gal. 5:1; Eph. 6:10-18; 2 Cor. 10:3-6; 1 Jn. 5:4

IN THE MASTER POTTER'S HANDS

My friend, as you yield your life to Jesus Christ, you will learn He is also the heavenly Father, God, Lord, and the Master Potter. The Potter molds His clay into His perfect image. As He takes you into His hands, you will begin a new and sometimes difficult process of change. You may doubt this renewing process is possible. You might say to Him, "How can I ever have the strength and ability to 'put it all down (change my life)' and become new for You?" Let your heart be at peace, for He has given you the power to believe that by His strength, you 'can do all things through Jesus Christ'. You must spend time in the Word. Then you will see that in the process, "The old has past away; behold, the new has come." As you seek a deeper and intimate relationship with Him; then, He will beckon you to place your sins (old behavior) and all your pain into the His hands. As you yield your soul and everything in your life to Him, you will see the process of a new 'walk with Jesus' is not as difficult as you thought it would be. As your love for the Master Potter deepens, you no longer need to walk in despondency or self-condemnation saying, "God, why did you make me like this?"

My friend, do not question the Lord's power to change you. Instead, listen to Him as you read His Word. Then, He will speak encouraging words to you. When you read Jeremiah 18, you will learn the Master Potter views you as if you are clay in His hands. You will find that the Potter reformed his clay (work of art) because it was marred and not what he intended it to be. Perhaps you think you still have the power to take your life into your own hands. Therefore, you wrestle to be what _you_ think you want to be. Dear one, please remember that the Master Potter has created you. Regardless of what you think, the Word says, since He created you, He has the power over you, the clay, to re-create (shape) you into His perfected image.

My friend, He desires for you to, willingly, offer everything about yourself to Him. That is so you will be like clay in His loving hands. It is essential for you be patient with this process. When you do, He will gently take you into His hands. Then, He will lovingly use every second of your life to shape you into what He created you to be. The potter's wheel spins around as He daily adds colors of joy and colors of darkness. That process represents every minute of pain and joy in your life. He will continue this process until He has perfected you into His image. Then everyone will behold His glory that is within you. Afterwards, people will see what He will do in the life of a simple 'lump of clay'. At that time, dear one, your transformed life will bring other people to Jesus. So, do not regret any transforming trauma you have endured, in your life.

Scripture References: Is. 29:16; Is. 45:9; Is. 64:8; Jer. 18:2-6; Jer. 32.27; Rom. 6:13, 16; Rom. 8:29; Rom. 9:20b-24; Rom. 12:2; 2 Cor.5:17

A FRIEND

This life, as we live it out, can go from joy, smiles, and victory to turmoil and defeat (ups and downs). God, in His infinite love, has designed each of us to be a brother or sister and a friend to one another in the transition of these. The Bible unfolds to you, two of the greatest examples of loyalty and devotion in friendships, ever told. These were through the friendships of Ruth and Naomi and David and Jonathan. After Naomi's husband and sons died, she decided to return to her homeland, in Israel. Her daughter-in-law, Ruth, chose to leave her family and country saying to Naomi, "Do not urge me to leave you or to return from following you. For where you go, I will go and where you lodge, I will lodge. Your people, will be my people, and your God, my God."

The book of Samuel gives you another model for a sacrificial bond of friendship. This was the bond between David and Jonathan. Jonathan was the son of King Saul. King Saul believed that David would take his throne and so he was determined to kill him. Because of the strong bond of the committed covenant and friendship between David and Jonathan, Jonathan forsook his devoted allegiance to his father and faithfully gave his all for David, in order to protect him from his father.

The Word tells us that a true friend will express the attributes of your heavenly Father toward you. He is, indeed, your truest friend. That friend will be compassionate, merciful, slow to anger, forgiving, faithful, trusting, patient, understanding, generous, and kind to you. This is especially during the times when you are suffering from immense discouragement. Dear one, it is truly an honor to find a cherished friend, such as this. The book of Proverbs gives us some examples of the characteristics, of a true and lasting friendship.

Solomon, the writer of Proverbs tells you that, "A friend loves at all times . . . ." He also assures you that ". . . there is a friend who sticks closer than a brother." This kind of friend will always love you and remain faithful to you, whether or not your choices and actions are in the direction of the Lord.

Your friend will seek you out to point you to Jesus. Jesus also stated in John, "Greater love has no one than this; that someone lay down his life for his friends."

In 1st Corinthians, the disciple, Paul portrays the qualities of a faithful, true, loving, and devoted friend:

"Love is patient and kind; love does not envy or boast; it is not arrogant or rude. It does not insist on its own way; it is not irritable or resentful; it does not rejoice at wrongdoing, but rejoices with the truth. Love bears all things, believes all things, hopes all things, endures all things. Love never ends . . . !"

In the book of Philippians, Paul said, ". . . but in lowliness of mind let each esteem others above themselves." Paul lovingly reminds you in Hebrews 13:5 that your best friend, Jesus, will never leave you. I ask you to purpose to demonstrate the quality of friendship, displayed in the Word, as you seek to follow the example of your greatest friend, your loving heavenly Father. When you are hurting and crying out in utter hopelessness, "I need someone to care," then a friend with the loving and compassionate heart of God will put their arms around you as they tell you, "I am here with an undivided heart and an understanding ear. I am here to show you that I care about what you are going through." A loving friend will tell you about their painful experiences. Then, they will share with you how God victoriously delivered them from their pain; so that you can know they truly relate to your emotional pain.

Friends: Linda, Connie, Tammy, & Katherine

That devoted friend is someone who will eagerly say to you, "See what my wonderful God has victoriously done for me." A genuine friend will love you when you come in aching despair, to say, "I am without hope. I feel that life is not fair!" They will love you if you come to them with a smile and say, "I have many good things to share."

They will seek the wisdom of God, so they can advise and teach you how to grow in His Spirit. They will never judge you; however, they will instruct you in His ways. Their committed friendship will demonstrate His love to you. By practicing the power of His love, they can share with you the truth about how a godly friendship should be.

At that time, you will see the qualities of the Lord, Jesus, through the power of the Holy Spirit in their life. A true friend will look for the best in your character and deeds, as they encourage you to reach out to Jesus. They will tell you all that He desires for you to be. A sincere friend will then encourage you not to give up. Next, they will tell you how to fight the good fight of faith! Last of all, dear one, when you are free from the 'things' that Satan has used to emotionally torment you; then, that friend will be someone with whom you can share a glorious and triumphant victory over Satan, the enemy. After that, you can show your friends and neighbors how much He loves them.

Scripture References: Ruth 1:16-17; I Sam. 18:3-4; 1 Sam. 19:1-7; 1 Sam. 20:1-42; 23:16-18; 2 Sam. 9:1-18; Prov. 17:17a; Prov. 18:24b; Prov. 27:9; Jn 15:12-13, 17; 1 Cor. 13:4-7; Gal. 5:22-23; Phil. 2:3-4

WE, A FRIEND OF GOD, AN EXTENSION OF THE LORD, JESUS CHRIST

(Let these words be the heart cry and desire of all those whom the Lord has 'set free')

Our greatest desire, as a Christian, should be to reflect the characteristics of our Lord, Jesus Christ, to a depraved world. He may bring people with many kinds of pain into our little corner of the world. Their pain could be emotional or physical. They could be weak and not strong, since their life seems 'all messed up'. Then, they need to see what Jesus' character looks like in us. This is so they will trust that He can free them from their 'hurts'. My friend, now, your task is to let Jesus' brilliant light of love shine toward them. Then, they will see His light of love for them. Therefore, each day, we will seek to keep a friendly smile on our face with Christ's joy in our souls, even if we have stress in our own life. Every day we will make a choice to use our voice, in order that we can bring hurting people to the Mighty Healer. Dear one, that Mighty Healer is Jesus. Only He can heal their hurts. They may be in our churches, our homes, our places of work, our market places, or elsewhere. We will ask Him to show us who they are. It could be that a burdensome disaster has caused great conflict to their souls. So, a feeling of 'gloom and doom' may weigh heavy on their hearts. Thus, it has left a toll upon their lives. Perhaps, Jesus has brought someone like that into your life. This could be the moment that He has given you to make a choice to use your voice to share Jesus' 'words of life' to them, instead of 'words of condemnation'. Sometimes we speak to hurting people with our own ideas for them. When we do that, we can cause more harm than good. Instead, we will portray the characteristics of the Lord, Jesus Christ, to those who are suffering from trauma in their life. They are patience, forgiveness, kindness, compassion, and wisdom.

Today, let us ask God for the Light of Jesus to flow into our hearts, so that we can be able to excel, in whatever task He would have us do. We will provide a listening ear to all those who choose to share the burdens of their aching and tormented hearts. In doing so, we may help someone else's 'load' to be a little easier. They will recognize that our love for them is genuine because He lives in us. We will act on what we believe. Then, we can truly be a light to people, in our little corner of the world.

Today, we will keep our thoughts solely upon the desires of the Lord, so He can use us as His vessels to comfort others who are suffering from difficult memories. We will share with them how the Lord has cast all our pain into the past. We can tell them because of His great love for them, He will also heal them of their pain. We will listen to people who feel Satan is tormenting them. Then we will pray for them. After that we will encourage them to 'fight the good fight' of faith in the Lord on high.

As we seek to help people with many kinds of needs, our goal is for them to feel, as if they are sitting around a warm, glowing campfire of God's love. A friend of God is a true bondservant of the almighty God, of the heavens and the earth. As we portray this to our friends, we will be a light in a dark world. At that time, we will raise up lamps of hope that all might see the glory of His majesty! It is then that God will get all the glory!

Scripture References: Ps. 133:1; Mt. 5:13-16; Lk. 10:29-37; Lk. 10:38-42; Lk. 19:2-10; Lk. 22:26-28; Jn. 15:15-17; 1 Cor. 10:32-33; Jas. 2:23b

WHAT IS THE TEST?

Which is the tree that has weathered the test of perseverance? Is it the tall tree that stood in the woods or the lone tree standing out in the field? The tall tree that has stood out in the woods is not the tree that has really stood the test. It is not the tree that stood in the forest deep that has really stood the test of perseverance, when 'twas' struck by the storm and snow and hail. The lone tree standing out in the field that has weathered every howling gale, when 'twas' struck by the storm and snow and hail is the tree that has really stood the test of perseverance.

The Christian woman who stands in a crowd of people and, with her comrades, lifts up her voice to let the world know what she believes, and of what things she has made her choice is not the one who stood the test.

The Christian woman who went to church, and there sang loudly and testified and let them all know that she was saved, happy and sanctified is not the one who stood the test. The woman who will stand alone, with real conviction, courage, and fervor, and lets the whole world know what she believes, and about those things, which are so real to her, is not the woman who stood the test.

But the Christian woman who stands alone, who has the Lord's joy and victory in the midst of perilous trials and is still blest with the rest from God and is evident that she lives the life of rest in the Lord before the world; that is the woman of God who has really stood the test.

A tribute chosen for my mother-in-law, Wanda Hall's, funeral; author unknown (she stood the test)

THE STILL SMALL VOICE OF GOD

My friend, if you have made the choice to believe that Jesus paid the sacrifice of death upon the cross for your sins, then you have given your life to Him. You, as well, have made a step of faith to enter into a covenant with your heavenly Father, who is the still small voice within your heart. That voice comes only through the shed blood of Jesus. Now, a new life begins for you. Even so, you may always have to deal with some oppression that comes against you. When you are facing the 'deep waters', you will believe that you have no control over the terrible incident in your life. This could cause you to feel weak, bewildered, and alone. Then, you could imagine you are drowning in the deep waters. You may say to Him, "Is there no comfort for my soul? Lord, will You please help me feel safe again? Is there no help for me? Do I not have a choice?" I ask you not to focus on being scared of the things that trouble you, for that may cause you not to hear His still small voice. Instead, think on the One who is the author and the finisher of your faith. Dear one, Jesus gives the ability to hear Him, to all those who believe that He died on the cross and rose from the grave to pay for their sins. If you have received the sacrifice of His blood upon the cross, you can also hear the still small voice of God. Now, take time alone and think about Jesus' great love for you. He knows all your needs, even before you tell Him. He knows you need His peace, comfort, encouragement, and instruction during your times of duress. Noah, Abraham, David, and many other servants of God 'stilled' their thoughts. Then they heard from Him. During your times of turmoil, you now, have the ability to hear and receive the comfort, encouragement, and instruction from the still small voice of God, just as they did. Our loving God also has a need. He eagerly waits for you to desire to listen for Him to speak to you. You cannot hear His voice, if you do not <u>choose</u> to set aside some quiet moments in the Word, in prayer and listening to Him.

Now, dear child of the risen King, imagine that you are sitting by the tree, on the shore of this beautiful lake, waiting to hear from the Lord, on high. I encourage you to wait with an eager heart, for Him to speak to your spirit. It is then that you will find both comfort and wisdom, as He speaks these words to you:

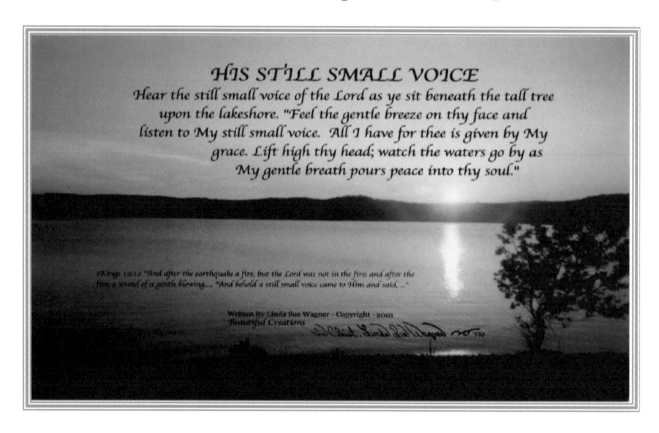

HIS STILL SMALL VOICE
Hear the still small voice of the Lord as ye sit beneath the tall tree upon the lakeshore. "Feel the gentle breeze on thy face and listen to My still small voice. All I have for thee is given by My grace. Lift high thy head; watch the waters go by as My gentle breath pours peace into thy soul."

1Kings 19:12 "And after the earthquake a fire, but the Lord was not in the fire; and after the fire, a sound of a gentle blowing.... "And behold a still small voice came to Him and said, ..."

Written By Linda Sue Wagner - Copyright - 2001
Beautiful Creations

Come, My child, sit in the shade and bask with Me, beneath the strong tall tree upon the green shimmering grass. As you feel the gentle breeze upon your face, I want you to remember that all I have for you has been given to you by My grace. Lift high your head and watch the clouds go by as you breathe out a sigh.

My child, I will speak to you in the soft whispering wind, from the beginning to the end. When you seek Me, You will hear My voice. I am pleased that you have made the choice to heed to My voice within your soul, instead of the voice of the enemy. So, be still, listen, and know that I am God. The still small voice within the depths of your soul is My Holy Spirit. Now, rest your head upon My shoulder and let Me quiet the distressed thoughts within your soul. I will not let all that rages against you have its toll upon you. I will give you the power to choose to be a mighty one that will not lose. I release into you a peace, which the enemy cannot take away. I will give you a strength never known to man. I will also pour wisdom and instruction into your heart to direct you, in all your ways. These attributes of My Holy Spirit will be with you, all through the night, and all through the day. My still small voice will be there to stifle all the things you dread, even in the eerie darkness of the night. The voice of My Holy Spirit will surround you with a comfort that is far greater than anything man has ever known. Then, I will show you what it is like for your soul to be whole and in deep rest.

At that time, you will wonder why you ever listened to Satan's voice of fear. My still small voice will be the only voice you will need to hear, throughout all eternity. I will comfort and heal all your pain. I will also draw you close to My bosom, because I desire your love and your presence. My child, I am delighted when you eagerly desire to bask in My presence, as you glorify and worship Me, at all times. My heart leaps with joy, when your greatest desire is to tell all the people whose path's you may cross, the good news of My salvation and how it can change their 'hearts', for the rest of their life."

Scripture References: Dt. 4:36; 1 Kgs. 19:12; Ps. 4:3-4; Ps. 5:2-3; Ps. 33:8; Ps. 46:10; Ps. 94:19; Is. 41:10; Jn. 10:3-4; Jn. 14:27; Jn. 16:33; Rv. 2:7

FROM THE GUIDING LIGHT TO THE MOUNTAINTOP

My friend, there are often questions in your life which seem to have no answers or purpose. Perhaps you have focused on your troubles with much concern. When you do, you might presume there is not even a reason for life, itself. If you think that, then you are choosing, only, to look at the <u>hindrances</u> which appear to threaten you. As you dwell upon them, you can become quite distressed. It can be hard to comprehend why this period of testing has come against you. That may be more than what you feel you can handle! I want you to know that Jesus (The Guiding Light) always has a reason for allowing every painful second of your life. This could be a time, when the heavenly Father will teach you His will through perseverance and patience.

Examples of nature will help you make sense of your disturbances, throughout each day. Anxiety and misery could cause you to perceive some of your burdens as being the most awful things that you will ever encounter. You could imagine that the waves of the oceans will seem too far to cross and so deep that your soul He cannot safely keep. Forests will seem too impenetrable. Valleys will seem so endless that you feel like you are treading on rocky paths that have no way out and no end. There could be rugged mountains that will seem too treacherous and too high to climb. You must pass through each strenuous terrain to reach your goal, which is the mountaintop.

You may think that you will find the way, which leads to peace, in your own strength (all by yourself). You cannot overcome those obstacles in your own strength! If you try, you will find exhaustion will creep deep into your mind. Then, everything will be like one giant struggle. Troubling occurrences will seem to 'lay heavy' upon your life. It is not possible to overcome these obstacles in your own strength. You will need His.

When these problems arise, you may feel like you are lost out on the sea. It is possible that some things can seem as overwhelming as the turbulent waves of the ocean. You might feel you will surely drown amidst them. <u>Jesus came to be the guiding Light</u> that will set you free from your pain and show you the way through each problem. As you trust Him, He will tell the waters to be still, so you will not be afraid. Then, His guiding light will help you see the dangers, which lie ahead on the troubled waters. Afterward, they will not swallow you up. He longs for you to seek Him to guide you safely to the shore.

Nevertheless, if you choose to 'chase after' your ideas of what is right; you will make your choices, rather than His. This can cause you a lot of pain and stress. After that you will, once again feel like there are turbulent oceans that are too deep to cross. Later, some complications may often appear to be like forests that are too dense for you to find your way through, to see Him. You could feel as if there are valleys that seem to have no way out, and high rugged mountains of troubles, which look insurmountable. Now, you can only utter a sigh of discouragement. After that, you will not be able to see His guiding light, which will lead you to your mountaintop of freedom. At that time, you may find yourself in the middle of things, which seem disastrous to you. Confusion can cause you to think, "How do I know which is the right path to follow to my mountaintop of freedom?" Then you can feel separated from the Guiding Light. I want you to realize that He will help you find your way to your glorious 'mountaintop of freedom' (tranquility in your thoughts).

If you turn back to God, He will guide your way across the ocean and cut down the branches in the forests, so you can see His guiding light above the forests. His Word will guide you so you can follow His choices for your life and not yours. Then, He will walk before you and smooth out the rough places in the valleys, which seem to have no way out. As you place your trust in the Guiding Light and follow His choices, He will lead you on His path, all the way to your mountaintop. However, dear one, you must seek His truth in His Word, and focus upon Him. If you do, He will walk with you through all that causes you to be so despondent. After that, hopelessness will surely, have to flee. Now, you can look ahead with hope, while He guides you across the oceans, through the forests, the valleys, and all the way up to the top of your mountain. His guiding light will give you His peace, faith, hope, and joy. Those attributes of the Lord, will help you to overcome every obstacle you must 'face'.

At that time, the tools of the Guiding Light will help you to triumph over every obstruction that Satan that will use, to keep you from reaching your mountaintop. After that, He will give you the force you need to fight and win the war against him. Subsequently, you will be able to conquer all your oceans, forests, valleys and mountains. You can, only, reach your mountaintop, with the persistence which comes from following the Guiding Light. As you depend upon Him (the Guiding Light), you will not stand at the brink of an ocean, which you cannot cross or a valley that is so long, you cannot safely pass through. Nor, will there be a forest so dense that you cannot see His guiding light shining through it. You will not stand and look upon a mountain too high to climb that you will be tempted to utter a sigh of fear. He will always guide you in the midst of all the grueling ordeals that you will encounter in this, sometimes, most intolerable life. When you follow the heavenly Father's guiding light, wisdom, and compassion, then, you can handle all your devastating hardships with God's leading and perception. You will have no need to fear what lies just beyond the next horizon, because God is always with you. He will use the 'light of His Word', (the Bible) to help you get through each crisis. When put your confidence in the Guiding Light, He will guide you to follow His path, in the midst of all your 'taxing' predicaments. Dear one, as you trust Him, He will help you make His good choices for your life.

You can now move forward with much expectation, since you have placed your trust in Jesus' guiding light. When you heart is devoted to Him, He will always protect you and strengthen you, in the midst of all the things, which you will experience. The Cherished One of the heavenly Father, of the heavens and the earth, wants you to realize that with His wisdom and compassion, you can now handle all your trials with God's positive point of view. If you utilize them, they will transform your life.

Then, you can know that Jesus has led you safely to the mountaintop above all that caused you to be distraught. Now, you can confidently say, "This is the day that the Lord has made; let us rejoice and be glad in it." Since, He has guided you to the mountain top, you can have a refreshed zeal for the Lord and His assurance of victory. Now, all will see the glory of God revealed by what He is doing in your heart.

Scripture References: Ps. 23:4; Ps. 32:8; Ps. 118:24; Ps. 119:105; Prv. 3:6; Is. 30:21; Is. 41:10, 13; Is. 45:2a; Jer. 32:17, 27; Mt. 17:20b; Mk. 4:39; Rom. 8:28; Rom. 8:37; Heb. 12:2; Jas. 1:2-4; 1 Pt. 4-7

IN THE MIDST OF YOUR DARKEST HOUR, LOOK BEYOND THE DARKENED CLOUDS

My friend, no one wants bad things to happen to them. It is natural to want good things to happen. Satan may deceive you into thinking life will be a 'bed of roses'. You may look up at the sky for a sign of beauty and hope for your life. Then, because of your feelings of gloom, you can only hear thunder in the darkened sky of your life.

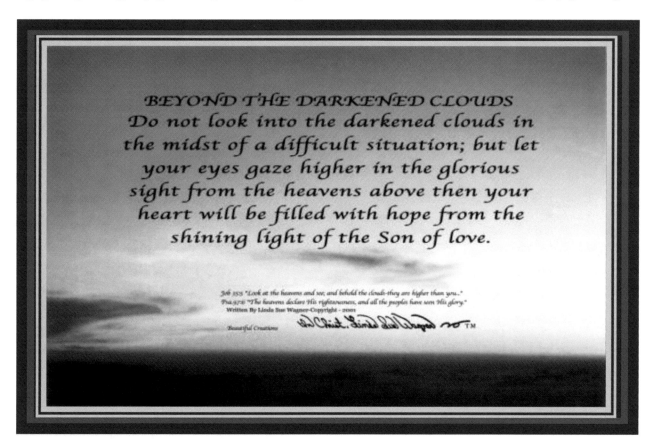

BEYOND THE DARKENED CLOUDS
Do not look into the darkened clouds in
the midst of a difficult situation; but let
your eyes gaze higher in the glorious
sight from the heavens above then your
heart will be filled with hope from the
shining light of the Son of love.

Job 35:5 "Look at the heavens and see, and behold the clouds-they are higher than you.."
Psa.97:6 "The heavens declare His righteousness, and all the peoples have seen His glory."
Written By Linda Sue Wagner-Copyright - 2001

Beautiful Creations

Despair may cause you to fail to see the <u>beauty</u>, which lies 'beyond the darkened clouds'. Dear one, Satan, (the tormenter) can cause the darkened clouds (bad times) to hover over your life. In this moment, you could feel as though they will bring you to your cowering doom. The oppressing dilemma might cause you to barely, have the ability to breathe a sigh. After that, you could think your darkest hour may be beyond what you feel you can tolerate.

Upon that point, you can be sure he will try to lure you into taking your mind off God and His Word. If he succeeds, you may make decisions by what you see with your eyes, rather than by applying God's words, in the Bible, to your predicament. Then, he will attempt to convince you that you cannot hear Him or sense His wisdom. If you feel like you are alone, then it can be easier for him to make you think you are 'cut off' from Him. When darkened clouds of doom seem to hover over you in your darkest hour, you may think there is no one to help you. At this instant, you might shout to Him in the midst of the darkened clouds, "I cannot see You working in my life. I need to know there is freedom and light beyond these darkened clouds!" My friend, if you are looking for the Lord to prove Himself to you; then, you will find He is, truly, there for you. If you ask Him to show Himself in the midst of your 'darkened clouds', He will do that.

He endured both physical and emotional suffering beyond anything you can comprehend, during <u>His darkest hour</u>. Thus, He understands your suffering, more than you can possibly imagine. He longs for you to look beyond the darkened clouds, so you can see Him moving them out of your life. He will speak these words from the Bible to you, "Then you will call upon Me and go and pray to Me, . . . I will listen to you. And you will seek Me and find Me, when you search for Me with all your heart. I will be found by you, says the Lord . . . ."

Now, I ask you to listen to the voice of comfort from the Lord, for He can bring beauty to your life, even

IN THE MIDST OF YOUR DARKEST HOUR:

"My child, I am the only One from whom your help comes. I will give you victory over all that Satan would use to destroy you. If you look beyond the darkened clouds of your darkest hour, I will fill your heart with overwhelming joy, comfort, and light. I will be by your side during your darkest hour, so you can see the beauty beyond them. It is then that I will remove your darkened clouds. I want you to know that I will never, no not ever, leave you, or forsake you."

Scripture References: Job 17:15; Ps. 34:4; Ps. 37:24; Ps. 46:1; 60:12

JOYOUS NEW SONG

My friend, there are days in which it seems like there is no end to the many burdens which are of great alarm to you. At times, they may be all at once; or again, they could be endless. Perhaps that could describe your life at this point. If this is true, you may wonder why you have to keep on walking through the 'valleys and the chaotic whirlwinds' in your life? You may not even be sure you can bear, yet another day of hardship. They could be so intense that you think the 'sun' will never shine for you, again. There are 'a lot of' days in which your storms (painful issues) will 'hang on' and cause you to doubt that this 'hard luck' will ever end. I can promise you, dear one, they will end in God's time. Maybe you have wept before the Lord saying to Him, "Where are You my Father and my friend? I feel so alone." I want you to know that you are not alone. He hears your cries. He is there even if you do not sense that He is near. In the length of your trials, you could feel like you are the only one who is duty bound to tolerate the long dark valleys and unsettling storms.

There are numerous people in the Bible who suffered countless periods, where their faith was tested. To expound on David's perspective, in the book of Psalms, during some of his traumatic times; He chose to trust in his heavenly Father, against all odds. It is of considerable significance to know that he sang joyous songs of praise to the Lord, during those most critical surroundings. That gave him a renewed strength and an enduring hope. In his times of turmoil, he found rest for his soul in the presence of the almighty God. Thus, he spent much time in the presence of the Lord. As David praised Him, he received a fullness of joy, which cannot happen without God. Nevertheless, God did not always remove the stressful attacks from his life. The tension of a demanding life is often, displayed in the lives of many people, today.

In the unpleasantness of pressures in life, many people may not experience the threat of death today. However, the suffering is still significant. God may not always remove your upsetting occurrences when you want Him to. At times, they will come on a daily basis. Do not despair, for He will lead you and strengthen you through the 'battles', which you must struggle with. Nevertheless, I want you to know, they will end in His time. Dear one, the Lord could choose to use these moments to draw you deeper into His endearing presence. Your heavenly Father longs for you to spend time in fellowship with Him in the quietness of your soul. As you spend time communing with Him, His love will spring forth into your heart. At that time, it will be as if it were a flowing river of living water (Jesus), *washing away your tears, from years of hardship* (Valley of Baca). *When your tears have vanished, you will sing and dance before the Lord, just as Miriam did, when the Israelites saw the victory their glorious God had given them. Therefore, rather than feeling miserable, I suggest you raise your hands up to Jesus, your victorious Healer. After that, you can choose to sing a joyous new song unto the Lord, even in the midst of your pain and weariness. At that time, you will receive a renewed strength, which will sustain you, just as it did David. Now, you can give Him thanks for the victory He so graciously gives you. When God is your shield, you will not grow weary from the battle. Only then, can you endure the dark valleys and the threatening disturbances in life, while He leads you through them each day. The Lord can give you great freedom from the emotional view of your most difficult environment. When He does, you will not be able to contain the freedom within your soul. You can now sing a joyous new song unto the Lord of the heavens and the earth. That joyous new song will ache to spring forth from your mouth, just as it did for King David, when he danced before the Lord. So, dear one, it time to shout, "Halleluiah, Jesus". I want you to know the Lord views it as an honor when other people watch you live out your convictions through your unwavering faith.*

When you do that, it will be because you choose to live your life with the Lord's great joy, perseverance, and courage. My friend, it is at this time, people will want to know what gives you such peace, joy, and strength. Now, the Lord gives you the unique opportunity to share your victory with others who are enduring such duress. They will gain great wisdom, as you tell them how you dealt with your past and present struggles. Then, you can surely rejoice in the Lord's abounding love, in the midst of your oppression and lengthy times of testing. My friend, your joyous new song will increase, as you tell them how your glorious God has brought you through your darkest valleys, turbulent storms, great unrest, and into your

GLORIOUS LAND OF JOY!

(Dedicated to Connie Adaire, my longest close relationship since 1988)

Scripture References: Ex. 16: 20-21; 2 Sm. 6:14; Ps. 144:9; Ps. 149:1

THE GREATEST WONDER OF ALL

The wonders of our great and mighty God are far beyond anything we could ever imagine. As you read His Word, I encourage you to search out the truth of His great love for you. God, the heavenly Father, loved all people before they were born. I ask you, "What is the greatest wonder of all?" It is my desire for you to understand that the greatest wonder of all was Jesus' birth, death, and resurrection. To comprehend this, it is critical for you to explore the beginning events of all God's creation. The heavenly Father and the Son created the first man and woman, Adam and Eve. God is holy, pure, and all wise. God absolutely will not tolerate sin. He deeply desires for everyone, upon the earth, to have a perfect relationship with Him. Yet, He said it could only happen as long as they did not choose to sin. Sin is disobedience to God (choosing to do wrong in the sight of God). The heavenly Father knew before He made Adam and Eve that they would sin. He also knew their sin would break their relationship with Him. This deeply grieved Him. He told them that their life would always be difficult because of their sin. Every person is a child of Adam and Eve; as a result, we inherited their sin nature (Their sin was passed on to us.). Thus, we still sin. God said that each of us must die to pay for our sins. He has a great love for all people. He longs for them to have the pure relationship that Adam and Eve first had with Him. Before they sinned, He had a requirement, which would restore the relationship of all people unto Him. For this plan to occur, God said that there must be a sinless blood sacrifice as the payment for the sins of everyone on earth. The Son of God was without sin. Therefore, He chose to send His own beloved Son, Jesus, to earth by birth, by a young virgin woman (miracle of all miracles), to be that substitute, the sacrificial lamb,' for everyone who would choose to repent of their sins. The prophet, Isaiah, confirmed that God would send His Son, Jesus (Immanuel), to earth.

The prophet, Isaiah, confirmed that <u>God would send His beloved Son, Jesus</u>, to Earth. He would come in the form of a babe sent from the Holy Spirit. He chose the virgin, Mary, to bare this child. Before Jesus was born, God chose Joseph to join with Mary in marriage to raise the child, Jesus, the Son of God. They were married and traveled to Bethlehem for the census. After traveling for days, they arrived in Bethlehem. Then, they sought a place to stay for the night. However, there was no room in the inn. In the midst of the night, Mary gave birth to the babe, Jesus, in the stable. She wrapped Him in swaddling, cloths and laid him in a (manger) *bed of hay.*

He was the Savior of the whole world. At that time, there were shepherds who were watching sheep, in a nearby field. An angel appeared to them in the sky. He told them that the Christ child had been born in the city of Bethlehem and said to them, "Fear not, for behold, I bring you good news of great joy that will be for all the people. For unto you is born this day in the city of David, a Savior (of the world), who is Christ the Lord . . . ." They went to Bethlehem and found the 'babe', Jesus, where the angels told them. The shepherds stood in awe as they saw this babe (the Son of God) lying in the straw. The angels from the heavens above sang, "Glory to the highest . . . ," in worship to their King. Later, there were wise men that had seen a new star, which foretold the birth of a new king of the Jews. They were searching for this King (Jesus) to worship Him. They followed the star from the east to find him. They traveled to Jerusalem in search of this King. King Herod heard about their search for the babe. His scribes informed him that Jesus would be born in Bethlehem. Therefore, he sent the wise men there to find the babe. He told them to come back to tell him what they found. That was because he wanted to kill Him. He thought that the 'babe' King, Jesus, would take his throne. Therefore, he did not tell them of his evil intentions.

The wise men traveled to Bethlehem, in search of the babe. As they looked up to the sky in the night, they saw the star over the house where He was living. They found him with His parents, Joseph and Mary. They humbly bowed down and looked upon Him in awe, as they worshiped Him. The wise men came bearing gifts of great wealth and presented them to Him. God told the wise men not to return to the king to tell him what they had found.

Later, the family moved to Nazareth where Jesus grew to be man. He was quite ordinary in appearance. He helped his father, as a carpenter. However, He was not just an ordinary man.

He was listening and asking questions of the teachers in the Jewish temple at the young age of twelve. As a child, Jesus had great knowledge of the biblical teachings. When he became an adult, He walked about the land and with the touch of His mighty hand, He healed the sick and the lame, gave sight to the blind, and restored hearing to the deaf. Then, the day came, when He knew the time had come for Him to become the blood sacrifice that His heavenly Father required, for the payment of the sins of every person who wanted to have their sins forgiven. In order for you to understand the greatness of His sacrifice for you, you must take a careful look at the last hours of Jesus' life. You will find the details of His birth, death, and resurrection, in the four Gospels of the Bible. God had already arranged a series of events that would lead to Jesus' crucifixion on the cross. The Jews wanted Him dead, so they used Pilate to carry out their plan to kill Him. The Roman soldiers arrested Jesus and brutally beat His body beyond recognition with whips of jagged pieces of metal that were attached to the whips. His flesh was literally, ripped from His back with each strike of the whips. They mocked Him with contempt. Later, they clothed Him with a purple robe and pierced holes into His head with a crown shaped with thorns. They 'gorged holes' in His wrists and feet with spikes, as they nailed Him to the cross. The crimson blood flowed down Jesus' body as He cried out to His heavenly Father, "Father, forgive them, for they know not what they do?" He suffered agonizing pain beyond the capacity of anything that we could ever imagine. This was entirely because the sins of all the people on the earth, weighed heavy upon His body. Because the sins were so great, God had to turn His face away from His beloved Son. At that time, Jesus uttered His last breath. He faced the cross with joy, for He knew He would conquer death and the grave through His resurrection. Consequently, the Savior victoriously rose up from the grave, in triumphant victory on the third day after His death!

This was so that He could offer the gift of eternal life to everyone on earth. However, in order for them to receive eternal life they would have to ask His forgiveness for all of their sins.

"For God so loved the world, that He gave His only Son, that whosoever believes in Him should not perish, but have eternal life. For God did not send His Son into the world to condemn the world, but in order that the world might be saved through Him. Whoever believes in Him is not condemned, but whoever does not believe is already condemned because He has not believed in the name of the Son of God.

This, my friend, is the STORY OF HIS GLORY!!!

Dear one, if you have not accepted Jesus Christ as your Savior, I ask you to consider this question, "Is there any room (in your heart) to let the Savior in?" Will you say, "Yes", or will you say that there is no room for Him in your heart (the inn)?" If you believe in Him and the price He paid for you; then, you can ask Jesus to be your Savior and submit your life to Him. He will forgive you of your sins, cleanse, sanctify, make you holy, and give you the gift of Eternal Life. After that, you can rejoice, knowing that you will spend Eternity with Him. He will also lead you in the paths of right, living. Now, your life will surely bring

GLORY TO HIS HOLY NAME!!!

HALLELUJAH!!!

Scripture References: Gn. 1:26a, 27; Gn. 2:7; Gn. 3:24; Is. 9:6; Is. 53; Mi. 5:2; Mt. 1:18-25; Mt. 2:12; Mt. 27: 54; Mt:28:4-7; Mk. 8:22-26; Mk. 9: 24-29; Mk. 15:1-39; Mk. 16:1-7; Lk. 1:26-37; Lk. 2:1-18;Lk. 23:3-5; Lk. 23: 20-24; Jn. 3:16-18; Jn. 5:5-14; Jn. 19:1-18, 30, 38-42; Jn. 20:19-22; 1 Cor. 15:3-8

VICTORY IN JESUS

Dear one, when you are going 'thru' relentless and colossal periods of gloom, it is quite possible to become disheartened. Satan will use these painful issues to cause anguish and weariness to your soul. At that time, you may cry out to your heavenly Father, "Why do you not show me the way out of the wilderness and lead me into my promised land? Have I not had my share of trials?" Moses believed God would part the Red Sea, and so; He did. Yet, the Israelites were still fearful, even after God parted the Red Sea. They continued in their fear, grumbling, insolence, and lack of faith in God. That caused God to let that generation wander in the wilderness for forty years. Thus, they suffered greatly and they never reached their Promised Land. It can be difficult to wait on Him, when you are in the midst of traumatic events. He may not choose, at this particular time, to reveal to you the easiest path to your promised land. He will use those trying episodes of suffering to mold your 'heart' to His perfect will, just as He did for them. Jesus said in the Word that He has come to do a <u>new thing in your life</u> (do you not see it?). Therefore, do not look at your, seemingly, impossible wasteland in dismay. You must realize that He understands and knows all your sufferings. His best for you could be that your victory will come with the joy He will place in your heart, as He renews your strength every moment. When He lived on this earth, He suffered far greater painful, emotional, and physical feelings, (humiliation and mockery) than you are or ever will endure. He knew why He was experiencing tribulation. God chose Him to take your place on the cross to die. This was so you would not have to die to pay for your sins. He knew His death had to be. That was because of the triumph He could see for you, as He walked with joy, all the way up Golgotha hill to the cross! When Jesus gives you the victory, nothing can permanently harm your spirit.

The Savior of all who believe and receive the sacrifice of His gift of salvation uttered not a word. That was because of the triumph He could see for you as He <u>walked with joy all the way up Golgotha</u> (Calvary) <u>hill, to the cross!</u> He knew His mission was complete by His resurrection from the grave. Other than salvation, the greatest victory you can have is to trust Jesus, amidst the emotionally demanding calamity in your life, just as John did. John, had great confidence in God when He said, "For, everyone who has been born of God overcomes the world. And this is the victory that has overcome the world–our faith. Who is it that overcomes the world except the one who believes that Jesus is the Son of God?" When Jesus spoke to His disciples, He assured them He would give them victory:

"'These things I have spoken to you, that My joy may be in you, and your joy may be full." "I have said these things to you, that in Me, you may have peace. In the world, you will have tribulation. But take heart; I, have overcome the world." "But thanks be to God, who gives us the victory through our Lord, Jesus Christ.'"

Dear one, you must wait patiently for Him (without complaining) to speak wisdom and comfort to you and heal your broken heart. After that, He can work out His plan in your life. It is not His will for you to look at your need in crumbling defeat. He desires for you to have victory over the evil, which has come into your life. You can, if you put your trust in Him. Next, He will walk with you and lead you through your wilderness, your storms, and all the way to victory. When you trust in Him, He will give you the grace to endure the 'rough terrain' in your life, with steadfast, unwavering, perseverance, and joy. The cross of Jesus will guide you safely, every step of the way, all the way to the 'top of your hill', through every crisis in your life. When Jesus gives you the victory, nothing can permanently harm your spirit.

63

So, do not look at your seemingly impossible wilderness in dismay as the Israelites did. Now, rejoice in the Lord, for there will always be a victory and a hope for you, through Jesus. My friend, He proved to you through His own suffering that He truly understands your pain. The light of His glory and the light of the cross will permeate your soul, every day of your life. If you will keep your eyes on the cross of your beloved Savior, then every day your victory will be won thru' in Him. When you walk in His light, you will never have to fear the storms Satan brings to your life.

Scripture References: Nm. 14:20-23; Is. 40:30-31; Is. 43:19; Jn. 15:11; Jn. 16:24b, Jn. 33; 1 Cor. 15:57; Phil. 2:14-15; Heb. 4:14-16; Heb. 12:2; Jas. 1:2-3; 1 Pt. 1:6-7; 1 Jn. 5:4-5

JESUS HAS BROUGHT YOU THE VICTORY

My friend, the enemy will always try to steal your joy. Regardless, you know that Jesus has given you His victory. Therefore, you can come to the Holy Spirit and say, "Come Holy Spirit. Wash my mind with the blood of the Risen Lamb. Let Your Living Water flow over me like a raging flood." When an evil thought comes straight out of the pit of hell and lurks its way into your mind; then, Satan can tempt you to think, "How am I going to find peace?" Instead, you must proclaim, "I am going to choose to think about Jesus." Then, you can lift up your hands to the 'Lamb', which was slain. You can do that since He has brought you the victory. You can know that it is now 'well with your soul', (serenity in your mind) because Jesus has resurrected from the grave and has given you a new life. Now, you are no longer in bondage to sin. The Word says that the blood of the risen Lamb gives you the power to stand firm, in your faith. Therefore, you can proclaim, "Greater is He that is in me than He that is the world . . . ." and as well, "For whatever is born of God overcomes the world. And this is the victory, (you see) that has overcome the world (even)–our faith." It is time to choose to 'stand firm in your faith'. When the battle seems up hill, you must take up your weapons and conquer the enemy, by the power of the blood of the risen Lamb. He has given you all authority over Satan. You can now say to the Lord, "I give You thanks for You have brought me to repentance. I will choose to rejoice, even in the battles." Dear one, God has the ultimate victory over all your painful experiences. It is in Him that you will have victory over sin and death. Now, you can joyfully dance in the valleys and on the mountaintops of life. After that, you can shout, "Thanks be to God; for His indescribable gift of grace!"

Scripture References: 2 Sm. 23:12; Ps. 59:5; Ps. 98:1; Jn. 1:29; Rom. 6:6; 1 Cor. 15:57; 1 Cor. 16:13; 2 Cor. 9:15; Eph. 1:7; Gal. 5:1; Heb. 12:2; 1 Jn. 4:4; 1 Jn. 5:4-5; Rev. 5:6; Rev. 12:11

I'LL NEVER FORGET THE LORD'S GREAT LOVE

I will never forget that when I walked through every trial in my life, it was my Lord, Jesus, who was holding my hand. I will never forget the physical and emotional pain that He suffered for me. He did that because He knew His death would remove the 'dross (sin)' in my heart. I will never forget the Lord's great love for me, as He took His last breath upon the cross. He walked to the cross of Calvary with joy, for He knew He would bring me to the place, which would show me His abounding grace and eternal glory. I will never forget that His loving choice to die on the cross would show me a greater love, far beyond anything I will ever know.

His merciful love has shown me that all the times of testing and all the emotional and physical pain, in my life, have never been in vain. When I think about His sacrificed and grief stricken body that hung upon the cross, I will never forget, "The Lord's Great Love". I will never forget when He spoke to me from the Word saying, "<u>I am the way, the truth and the life. No man comes to the Father, but by Me.</u>" I will always remember the Lord's great love, because He came to earth to save all those whom the enemy has lead astray. I will always shout joyfully, "<u>For me to live is</u> (in) <u>Christ, and to die is gain.</u>" From the beginning of time, there has never been a love like 'The Lord's Great Love!'

Scripture References: Ps. 138:7; Ps. 139:5; Is. 30:21; Is. 41:10; Is. 43:1-3; Is. 58:11; Heb. 13:5; Jn. 14:6; Jn. 19:16-30; Eph. 1:7; Phil. 1:21

WHEN I AM FAITHLESS, HE IS FAITHFUL
"Footnote to the Reader"

I did not write this book to tell how well I stood the test in all the difficult and painful hardships, in my life. It was not to tell how great my faith in God was, in the midst of my many unbearable experiences. There were times when I was not faithful to God during these trials and tribulations in my life. I have not always stood the test. Many times, I just 'hung on to God for dear life'. There were moments that I did not think God was even there. I have written this book so I could tell you about God's love, power, and faithfulness, in the midst of often-horrific emotional and physical pain. As I look back on all my difficult situations, my heart grieves, for there were times, which I did not faithfully trust God to help me deal with the pain, by relying on His peace, joy, and faith. There were periods in my life in which my heavenly Father must have shook His head in sadness, as He watched me blunder through some situations without even reaching out to Him. However, because HE IS AN AWESOME GOD OF GRACE, He never judged or condemned me; nor did He ever, let go of me! Praise God! In the midst of my tears and my grumbling, He was always there to listen to me and have compassion on His sometimes, faithless child. There were often times, all I could say was, "Lord, just give me grace". Each time, I learned to 'hold on to Him' tighter than the time before. I know this book is truly from God, because I am just a very simple farm girl, with only a high school education and a couple years of secretarial vocational school over 30 years ago. I endured numerous 'hard knocks' in life, just like many others have. Now, friends, I can declare, Jesus is faithful to us all and, once again, this is only the beginning of the journey all the way to the top of the hill, to the
GREAT AND GLORIOUS LAND OF JOY!

My friends, "Lastly, I must tell you to never, never give up, because Jesus is right by your side, with His outstretched hand. As He holds out His hand, I beckon you to place your hand into the loving Savior's hand (and hold onto Him for dear life), throughout all eternity and 'fight the good fight of faith through Him!!!'"

ENDING ENCOURAGEMENT

My prayer for you is that after you have been healed from all your pain, that you will be able to minister, out of your pain, to other hurting people, just as Paul encourages you in 2 Corinthians 1:3-7.

"Blessed be God and Father of our Lord, Jesus Christ, the Father of Mercies, and God of all comfort, who comforts us in all our affliction, so that we may be able to comfort those who are in any affliction, with the comfort with which we ourselves are comforted by God. For as we share abundantly in Christ's sufferings, so through Christ, we share abundantly in comfort, too. If we are afflicted, it is for your comfort and salvation, and if we are comforted, it is for your comfort and salvation, and if we are comforted, it is for your comfort, which you experience when you patiently endure the same sufferings that we must suffer. Our hope for you is unshaken, for we know that as you share in our sufferings, you will also share in our comfort."

May God bless you as He washes away your pain and sets you free from all the things that you fear. Now, do you know what is really, wonderful? You now have the key for unlocking other prison doors, so other people also might be set free!!!

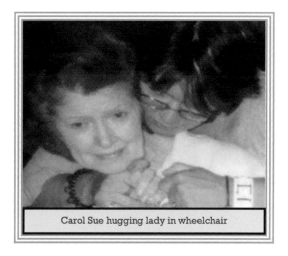

Carol Sue hugging lady in wheelchair

CPSIA information can be obtained at www.ICGtesting.com
Printed in the USA
BVIW122341220519
549012BV00016B/5